FROM THIS DISTANCE

FROM THIS DISTANCE

Poems by Susan Snively

MIDDLEBURY COLLEGE LIBRARY

ACKNOWLEDGEMENTS

Some of these poems first appeared in *Poetry, The American Scholar, The Second and Third Berkshire Anthologies, The Massachusetts Review, The Kenyon Review, The Threepenny Review,* and *Ploughshares.*

Copyright © 1981 by Susan Snively
All rights reserved.
Printed in the United States of America.

Typeset by Jeffrey Schwartz
Paste-up by Ed Hogan / Aspect Composition
Cover painting by Mario Caluori
Cover photograph by John Howard & Thomas Jacob
Cover design by Mary Rothenbuehler

I wish to thank my husband Jim, Robert Hahn, and Jean Grossholtz for their encouragement, and the Massachusetts Artists Foundation for a Fellowship which helped me to complete this book.

Library of Congress Catalogue Card Number 80-70831
ISBN 0-914086-35-9

The publication of this book was made possible with support from the Massachusetts Council on the Arts and Humanities, a state agency whose funds are recommended by the Governor and appropriated by the State Legislature. This project was supported in part by grant from the National Endowment for the Arts in Washington, D.C., a federal agency.

Alice James Books are published by
Alice James Poetry Cooperative, Inc.

Alice James Books
138 Mount Auburn Street
Cambridge, Massachusetts 02138

in memory of Sarah Youngblood

CONTENTS

APPROACHING THE SUBJECT

MYSTERIES

APPROACHING THE SUBJECT

THE CHAMBERED NAUTILUS OF EDWARD WESTON

(from the *Daybooks*)

      The shells stand all night
waiting for the camera
      windows are closed against wind
the photographer waits for morning
      warning his child not to run
but the cardboard backdrop slips
      from the movement of a cat or a passing truck
and disarranges them
      Sweating and angry, he hides under the cloth
finds "the slight change an improvement"
      an act the gods intended
When he is not taking pictures of shells
      he watches a woman dance
"not a photographer but a spectator"
      she dances nude
Later he enlarges his prints of her
      to life size
but erases her name from his journal
      and the words he found for her body
The shells move in the night
      having their own arrangements
Focusing again, he asks them
      how they want to be, and
they give him what they know

SKY ABOVE CLOUDS

(for Georgia O'Keeffe)

She knows, looking from the plane window
        that this far up, the view from above
is the same as from below:
        blue space massed with clouds
as if the clouds were mirrors, showing
        themselves in infinite series
impossible to limit
        to the fixed, stretched canvas
The clouds are oblong & regular
        stylized arrangements of distance, which dim
as they move to the horizon
        with that sure-footed sight
of travellers in planes, longing for space
        & when we, grounded, look at the painting
she made on earth of the sky
        we say first, oh it is the sky, & then
realize we have risen as we looked,
        risen in our slips of ice
toward the vision
        there is nowhere to go beyond.

16

APPROACHING THE SUBJECT

(O'Keeffe paints a jack-in-the-pulpit)

She said, "I will make them see what I see
though if I painted it real
I would have to paint it small."

       The flower filled the canvas,
       green waves falling
       from the edge to a center
       blue-black, a rod, a tower
       struck by lightning white—

the center of the world
she approached slowly
to free the pistil from its cassock,
show its halo like unstruck
fire in a match head.

BONES I

"I have tried to paint the Bones and the Blue."
                    —Georgia O'Keeffe

Always, when I looked, you were there,
"seen and not seen as such things can be."
When I went out on the mountain
to fish, I found and brought you home
knowing I would use you someday.
                    And when
I picked you up again
you had not changed. The holes
in the pelvis were familiar
showing the light through
like the wildness of the sky
in my own flesh,
                    continually found and lost
as the bones, the swift bones of the head
curve upward from the skull shell
out of mind.

BONES II

Always more sky than earth
in the world.
             Can you get there
             from here, through the holes in the bones,
             the charged sockets of the eyes
             through which the blank page
             shines like the sun?

Antlers crown the mountains.
The points of the horns
cramp like fingers
around empty air
             and here is a flower, an eye,
             a red wash of hills
             arranging the infinite

that circular ruin
of the faraway nearby,
of the blood the bone.

SUNDAY

Boats come into the harbor
carrying the sea in their long nets
the nets are grey & woven with seaweed
like the hair of an old forgetful woman
we cannot tell if it is morning yet

Small birds run into the water
run back from its leaping feet
a dead jellyfish sweats in the tide
the moon tugs at our feet
we belong in the kingdom of extremities

You run after birds with a camera
the water runs after the birds, the wind
runs after the water, the moon chases
the water inland On the prow of a distant boat
water is breaking like a shell

The wind rains sand on us, atoms of shell
& bone, drops of blood & salt
under the sea the dead rain down
on the living & the living swim up
into the graven lenses of our eyes

We have been here a long time
Animals are coming forth from the sea
on tentative limbs
hunting the sun Our footprints disappear
over the edge of the world

FOR A PAINTING OF A WINTER BARN

I have laid each stone strictly
over the tight spaces of my emptiness.
When I count them, my eyes clear,
though the sky bears the cataract of winter.

Slate tooth, stone lip,
the barn roof hunches in heavy weather.
Its profile shocks the air into quiet.
Bent weeds shiver and still.

This is the difficult landscape
where nobody's eye is welcome.
Here is no white drift, clean and pristine—
only a dog-track frozen in a furrow.

How the snow mottles and appalls me.
Left-over wheat perforates the ice.
I cannot catch hold:
my eyes slip, blearing,

though a glaze of tears seals them from wind.
Things that survive are hard:
the hay-rake, whose spokes prick the air,
the weathervane, turning ceaselessly.

I am blunt, unrecognizable,
having nothing to do with the cold
but to lift a thin brush in thin air
and set it down: necessity, hunger.

BRUEGHEL IN 500 PIECES ("CHILDREN'S GAMES")

An artist put us together, an artisan cut us apart.
Our games are your puzzle: you must make whole people
out of limbs and boots and split faces.

The smile of the fat burgher does not match
the grin of the cow-girl, the pot-boy or the tailor,
though for an instant two strangers seem to fit,

shoulder to cheek, who cannot meet when all
our citizens are ordered to the square.
Now, from part of a house, part of a man sings into nowhere.

On the left, heads surface in the river, while
a drunk sleeps in sunlit green. Piece by piece,
a field seizes the distance, the city takes hold.

Houses too, brown and predictable,
solidify, and faces bloom out of petalled skirts
twirled in a dance. Active, we are more elusive:

we all look alike and not alike,
round faces, round bodies like Dutch jugs.
Some have fat smiles, some wear red hats—

we can do marvelous things with ourselves.
Can you, bent to your compulsive eye,
sport and tumble in the horse-trodden dirt

like one of these strangers? Do you know what it is
to roll over and over in front of everyone
with your skirts lifted, laughing?

Doubtless, you say—noting our geometry
as we fill the square with motions
that look like nonsense and yet make sense—

we are handled by some higher power
who says, you with the wine jug, over here,
and you with the red hat, over there.

We do not mind. He has played with us,
and is with us now, if you can find him.
When he lifts his brush we call a holiday:

he gives us our freedom, which he arranges
into circular games, square dances.
You who are fitting us into each other

are nevertheless not in control. You with the red eyes
who have stayed up all night with us
as if to revive some game you have lost—

we would ask you into the square if we could,
were it not that something has seen fit
that you sit working, with lines in your face.

DUST

When they opened me there was a smell of flowers—
delphinia, olive leaves, berries of nightshade
which crumbled like skin, giving off fragrance
as the centuries leaped into the air.
My flesh had joined my bones,
rotted by dried unguents, stuffed with linen.
I have become my own buried kingdom.

The boat never comes, the bird flies away
into the sun, and the sun disappears
under a lid of gold and glass. Long since
I have put aside my gifts: the slings and bows,
the diadem, the chariot of wine. In eternity
you hear the sound of water like an endless song
sung by your mother before you were conceived.

If you become a temple, you will be an eternal mystery,
dark eyes under a cloak of stone,
moving through history like a heavy ghost.
What was my life? On a painted chest
my queen is stroking my shoulder with balm.
In an alabaster jar
lies the burnt remnant of my heart.

They went back through the long tunnels, leaving prayers
to seal my dead city. Under the wind and sun
the sand heaves silently. O God, I am but a little space,
a nest of dead wings. . . .
You who open my soul, remember me in my youth,
even as I was on the day I was born,
hastening toward death on golden feet.

MOVING

A tribe of Persian nomads with no laws
but the laws of the land: their life is so simple
it cannot be understood
Their herds of goats follow them / milk
for yogurt, skin & bone for cradles & spoons
The men choose the cousins they will marry
& marry them / The women are abased,
waiting to eat or for a decision to be made
Everywhere they arrive they have been before
Their minds move silently around an empty
space they would call home
if they could remember

The afflictions of the tribe are not recorded
because the first is blindness
& the second is the loss of words
The first is caused by the sun, the second
by too much travel / A man will wake up sightless
on strange ground & think it is his home,
the valley of his ancestors / From that day
he must wear a leper's bell & go with the goats
A woman will discover
after years of waiting, that
she wants to tell stories
The husbands are blind & must not
be deserted / The women have much to tell
of their wandering, but to do so they would
have to stop they would forget
what they had to say

FABLE

The man & his wife have decided
the girl must not know they know
she is in love with him
I am beginning in the middle of this story
It started long ago & there is no
end to it / I have been all its
characters at least once:
the wife who pretends to be concerned
the helpless object of someone's love
the confused heroine
You can combine us in all ways
but the result is always the same
the event which resists its telling
or the event which did not happen
There are two other parts
to the story: one which
takes place on a street in a
foreign city / The girl & the man
have agreed to meet for lunch / He was
supposed to buy a present for his wife, but
could not find what she wanted / When he
says her name, the girl feels sick though she
knows she is still loved at that moment
Later she torments him by trying to jump
in a canal / The other part is years later,
the girl has become a wife who hates
not her husband but all other
wives who mirror her eventual defeat
at the hands of herself or of
some girl, alone & brilliant
as she used to be / Meanwhile she gathers in
lovers for safety & friends for hiding

but secretly dares the impossible
in her mind, with impossible men: Maybe
this time she will get it right, break the glass
coffin, cut through the hedge
of briars or find how the dead frog
poisoned the well / Maybe not
I am not going to tell you the end
of the tale, but here is a clue:
There is an old woman who lives in her shoe
who has all the answers / She is real,
you can believe in her, there
is nothing she does not know
but there is one catch
She will punish you terribly
if you do not tell her
everything.

TRYING NOT TO TELL YOU GOODBYE

Knowing that it starts in me
I keep back the pain I want to tell you:
how I watch your mind growing wings
and imagine my fistful of feathers.

You are the gentlest man I know
and I know you only in your gentleness.
This is the singular fact that scares me
since the air around you is full of power

and you regularly dream of flying
into some startling updraft.
Since you are as free as you are kind
you could go off at any moment,

your backward glances full of love
falling around me like confetti.
I am trying to tell you how it is
to be a woman who knows these things

who knows that knowing will make no difference
unless it starts in me again and again,
love like a windy tree in the sun
bearing the *chiaroscuro* of our lives.

FROM THIS DISTANCE

Your hand on the shotglass, shaking;
through smoke, your eyes asking the question

to which I said *not yet*
and later *yes* and now *no* again

When you didn't ask with words
was it because you had said them too often

or never said them enough?
And when I didn't disclose my final answer

was it to keep the fantasy complete
which we knew would disappear

one day, quietly, like this?

The house, opening up for the summer

is bigger, windows dense with leaves & light,
lilac-sprays grouped in glasses;

everything seems possible.
A visit might be carefully arranged:

the night just cool enough for a fire;
certain words would break from us

tethered at one end
to fly toward the body & nowhere else,

That sensible object,
the given in the world that takes away. . . .

Distance used to give us scenes like this
we looked across as across a dining table

cleared now, polished & reflective,
dusted by a blown window curtain.

Long ago, knowing what I would say
but not knowing how

I thought, it started with this:
your hand shaking

its silent imperative:
Because you mean something

it is something if I let you go.
Sitting still, I kept my eyes steady,

transformed into the *something* meant—
a flower, a fish, a bird

bearing the name of a goddess
whose name, in turn, meant

bird, fish, or flower.

Now the distance seems natural,

its quiet the quiet of summer evening
where a few anonymous cars pass

one hears but does not listen for.
I move in the twilight from room to room,

through a house emptied of furniture,
looking for pennies, fingerprints, smells,

opening a door
to a room where the fire was

& seeing no charred logs, no ashes
but the clean grate

like an open palm
from which nothing is missing

because nothing was taken.

THEIR FOOT SHALL SLIDE IN DUE TIME

—Jonathan Edwards

Edwards said we may go out of the world
    suddenly at any moment, when God
        pours his words before us & they freeze

On roads, on bridges,
    new cold skin is laid on, flayed off
        by the wind's whipping sentence.

Driving, I hold my foot back:
    in due time it will slide
        whatever my hands do.

There is no evidence
    my next step will keep me here
        on this white, ecstatic edge

over which water rushes & stops
    in blue ice, & falls
        unmelted, of its own weight.

Edwards burned & froze
    in his dry ice interdictions
        not knowing how he knew the world

through the soles of his feet
    printed with the shapes of the earth
        like plants struck in rock.

At any moment, caught in two worlds,
    he would inhale the wind
        & breathe out ghosts

a phantom audience
    of the many who had gone before
        easily into the mouth of hell.

The arbitrary forms of his words
    hang in the trees like wet snow
        packing the branches;

in due time they will slide
    off, showing the tree
        blacker & wetter in new light.

Ice-flakes riddle the air.
    Star-forms stiffen
        in the window,

a little universe
    I bear before me, moving
        in my own time, while

love like a fast creek
    flows, tuned
        to the changes in the air.

Would Edwards have said, like Edgar,
    your life is a miracle
        to one who climbed an imaginary cliff?

The ground is *a rotten covering*.
When the wheels slip
I turn into the skid

strangely happy at that moment
suddenly out of the world, saying
hello & goodbye in the same breath

the black trees & the white
sky turning   thinking
this is supposed to be.

WAIT

—sign above Kafka's desk

(for Robert Hahn)

Good whiskey, neat, can break
the ice. At the bottom of the glass
there are words you must get to, but
they can wait. You lean back,
resting your head full of syllables.

Faces of people you have loved
swim toward you briefly
then retreat, older suddenly
in the approaching shade.

Nothing to do now
except obey the singular law
of the poet's lawless life:
to love people,
to see them go

and then to go inside, while the evening
still looks like the afternoon,
before it is too late,
and begin:
shutting a door to the rest of the house

thinking of the books to be accomplished
and the poems in them, unavoidable now,
factual as children
who speak the truth.

ELEGY FOR SARAH

Dickinson wrote to a preacher
about Ben Newton,
wanting to know how it was at the end,
if he had seen a passage
to another world
not forbidden to her.

"Called back" her last words,
disputed by theologians.
Did she realize, as she walked
out of the end of her life,
that she had always been walking back
toward her own calling voice?

And that when she arrived
at the hour, it would be
like sitting under a tree
whose yellow leaves would fall
perfect, one by one,
until her lap was full?

When you died
there was an hour left of daylight,
pink and yellow in the summer haze.
I was driving west,
passing a slow truck,
my life mute and peaceable as water.

What did I expect?
You would have said
that is it, the lifting of a curtain,
a leaf dropping from the jade plant.
I am writing
as if you were here to agree,

as if you were here to say
what do you want to happen;
what is your mind for
if it cannot occupy itself
as if furnishing a room
with fine, perishable things?

DESIGNING THE LIGHT

When you can't sleep, words are always there
to tell you why and keep you still awake
finding more words to send you back to sleep.
Waking into the yesterday of morning,
you think of the first thing that you have to say
to put the light in place.
                              You want a drink—
no, not the redeye of a redeyed writer
who bucks in the saddle of his daily chore,
but something a million people might be drinking,
to join you in their fellowship of work
and weary cameraderie: *Good coffee,
it looks like snow / a day to stay indoors,*
some words to keep words safe, or set them going
like toy cars in a grooved, metallic track
while you watch them go around and around and back.

The faces greet you. Do the faces matter
or the mild heads to which they are attached?
You'd like to think there is no difference
between an open eye and its interior.
You'd like to walk unblinking in that space,
clearing a path through complicated shadows,
but as usual, you pause at the door too long.
Today you're tired. Perhaps you'll let yourself
loose on the graven byways of your childhood,
a myth you filled with books, and watch their eyes
watching your eyes to see what they are filled with.
You think of Jane Eyre waking from her fit
seeing the *red glare crossed with thick black bars.*

The image when you read it was no image;
there were no words to say just what it was
except itself. You saw it when you shut
your eyes, the red blinds pulsing with a vein
which bled with all the colors in the spectrum
until it blackened and you woke again. . . .
Afraid of yourself, you start with someone else,
a critic who knew and never knew the author.
How can you say what you were at her age?
The chalk dispels you: *hunger, rebellion, rage.*

A character you encountered in a novel
(forbidden reading, sandwiched between the papers
and trips to fix the car) kept her tongue going
all day describing everything she saw
and everything she did—birds, weather, shit,
the taste of parsnips and of her own mouth,
the sounds of neighbors groaning in their tents
and little lives stirring among the leaves.
Reading the book, you laughed, thinking of Whitman
throwing his scroll of particulars into space
and stepping on it toward infinity—
what have you thought of today besides today,
or have you really thought about the present,
or is it something you can think about?
You wish you were in charge of a real something,
a box of fish, or a terrarium,
even a loaf of bread, whose life would last
as long as you gave a mind to it, and whose death
would be no greater matter than its life.
Everything you touch has a life of its own
which you fear to touch and chill it to the bone.

Afternoon. You trudge a whitening path,
the flakes like whispers falling across your back.
The clouds have left a broken crack of white
through which the sunset pours a wash of purple.
Your carven soles publish your sober footprints,
briefly the snow refills them, one by one.
It is a comfort to be thus erased,
like looking up at stars and stars and stars.
If the path lasted, you could go on forever,
the words at last falling away like snow.
But you walk until the pathway turns to gravel
which makes you have to hear where you are going,
correcting the sentence which began with *but*,
starting again with a more definite object.
A streetlamp stands before you, and a white house,
luminous in new paint, with dark green shutters
and a dead garden and two snow-filled swings.
You love the friend who lives here. Looking up
at a darkened window, glossy with black light,
you live for a blessed instant with no words,
not even *love,* not even aware of thinking.
The streetlamp hums its glow into the air;
the white flakes, quieting, seem to hang suspended
like dust motes in the dome of a cathedral.
And now you move on, your right arm weighted down
with something you are carrying.
                              Heading home
slowly, you forget to remember where the day went.
On your wrist the watch ticks the same minute twice
and now you think of a poem you'd like to write
which begins *when you can't sleep* and ends with *light.*

MYSTERIES

FOR THE THIRTEENTH WIFE

(Susan Snively, 13th wife of Brigham Young)

Your name, my name, under the little picture
stuck in the lineup of the Prophet's women.
Yours is a plain face among plainer faces—
the hair flat to the head, the middle part
white and straight like a highway through the salt flats,
the skin starched and beaten like a collar. . . .

Married at thirty-one, you bore no children.
Even your anniversary was plural:
Susan and Ellen, Martha and Maria,
four at one blow, in Nauvoo, Illinois,
St. Agnes' Eve, the twenty-first of January.
You were a Southerner, "Young's Virginian wife,"
"modest" and "kind," "aggressive," "energetic"—
even the adjectives print different pictures
with the dull keys of different clichés.
At thirty-one, what had you given up
to travel westward with a thousand Mormons,
a thousand oxen, seven hundred cows,
horses, dogs, cats, five beehives and a squirrel?
Safety in numbers, on the overland trail.

Heaven grew larger as you travelled toward it,
but then the numbers seemed to crowd you out,
your very name forgotten in the list.
The sun, rattling its way across the sky
day after day, and gliding down at dusk
into its easy notch between the hills,
mocked your slow footsteps. You could not protest:
talking made thirst, and water was for cattle.
Wakened at night, you thought you heard God calling,
his voice an echo passed around the stars.

You lay awake to listen for your name,
heard it at last, called in the roll for breakfast.

"For eight years, Susan Snively lived alone
four miles away from all the other wives
at the Farmhouse, where the Prophet would send a woman
to supervise the butter and the cheese.
After these years of solitary labor,
Susan returned in poor health to the Lion House."

Standing on the verandah of the Farmhouse
and watching the Prophet's carriage roll away,
you may have thought yourself at last a wife
ready to shape her days around her labor.
The brand new house, with walls made of adobe,
the forty-foot kitchen, hundred-and-fifty acres
of pine, mulberry bushes, corn and wheat
tilled by the thirty laborers in your charge—
it might have seemed a kingdom in a kingdom,
and your own work to feed the multitude
a daily miracle, renewed at dawn
as if your buttered hands prepared the sun. . . .
The forty cows made milk, the thirty men
took bread into the fields and brought back wheat,
the churn could not be stopped. You thought of children,
the little ones who did not know their father
except as a face at one end of the table,
a hand to ring the bell, a ponderous voice,
and eyes that always looked above their heads.
What would the children eat if you stopped churning
and strayed into the locust trees, and lay
down in the thorny grass and shut your eyes?

At last the Lion House, a top floor room,
gabled, with its own fireplace. Twenty chimneys

could let the neighbors know in scrolls of smoke
how many wives were living with their husband.
Alone in your room, accustomed to aloneness,
you listened to others dressing in their rooms
and going down to breakfast.
                                              Only one,
the newest wife, whose name was Ann Eliza,
would climb the stairs, bringing a glass of milk
and settle at your feet to tell her troubles:
Harriet's wrath, the rancor of Amelia,
the lonely vigil for the absent husband,
her children swept up in the multitude.
Day after day, talking with Ann Eliza,
it seemed you never could fill up the years
that you had lost to silence—even now
you had to pause so frequently for breath,
and there were many voices in the halls.
You shared a nightmare of eternity—
a hall of rooms, and in each one a woman
waiting for footsteps coming and retreating
and wondering whose door displayed the chalk mark.
You thought that others might have dreamed the same,
your minds coordinated, like your menses.

Two women whispering in a house of whispers,
you knew that in the lives of other women
there had to be a secret way of speech
under the words intoned at evening meals
which sent your wishes where you could not go,
like the last wish you told to Ann Eliza
the rainy day before she ran away:

"How I should like to ride out in a carriage.
And how it would do me good to see the country!
He never lets me ride."

WOLVES

Freud's famous "Wolf-Man" case is a history of a childhood nightmare: its sources in fairy tale and the experience of the primal scene, witnessed by Freud's patient, an exiled Russian nobleman living in Vienna. Freud left Vienna in 1938 and died in London in September, 1939. The "Wolf-Man" remained in Vienna through the war and lived to write his autobiography.

THE WOLF-DREAM

Outside the window, a tree
looms with five white wolves.
The window flies open. The child
is suddenly awake
though he sleeps, dreaming white
wolves on snow, in a grey forest of fears.

Later he will narrate his fears:
the broken walnut tree
at Christmas, spread with white
bedclothes, hung not with gifts but wolves,
while he dreams he must lie awake
forever, a feverish child

doomed to be always the child
hiding in the man, the man in his fears.
Nightly, yearly they come. *Awake*:
on the glass the dry finger of the tree
scratches and summons. *Here are the wolves,*
your parents, your loves. The hot sheets are white,

the long afternoon is white
with fever and love. The child
dreams pictures of wolves
striding and smiling. Fears
rustle in his head, the tree
grows larger and he jerks awake

to see what he must see. Awake,
his parents are tangled in white
flesh, his father erect as a tree,
his mother bent like a beaten child
but smiling. She has no fears
of what she has devoured. The wolves

are only picture-wolves
in books. Yet they are always awake
under the covers. He knows and fears
what lies under the white
sheets, snows, nightclothes. He sees the child
looking at the tree

and knows he will look until he cries, cry
until he talks himself awake
to begin the history of his dread.

WOLFWORDS

We eat your precious kids,
hide slobbering in your beds

all day, tricked out in drag,
counting our tender victims by the bag.

The white flank, the red orifice
we know like lovers: that sweet piece

Red-Cap and her sour granny
licked with flattery like honey:

goatlets, yellow
and bony, we can swallow

six at a gulp. The maw
is our mind and mindfulness the law

which governs appetite
and ghosts whole villages overnight.

For these imagined crimes, you will sew stones
in our guts. Our moans

will be your nightmusic, our white coats
will ruffle on the backs of Sybarites.

O You
who speak words and know they are not true,

we have no use
for the bodies you worship and abuse.

Your hamstrung arms
and legs, your heads full of dreams,

brooding and hopeless in your sleep:
what would we do with them? You are like sheep,

you are like pigs
in houses made of jewelry and twigs,

the stuff of nightmare fires. We watch you run
inside. We turn our backs.
                              The sun

behind us makes our shapes
long and black on the long white steppes,

we travel slowly. It is true
that when we sleep we dream of you,

but not as you surmise.
We are as sad as you are, twice as wise.

The way
we know is with our blood, for blood can say

what men will try
with beasts they carry in their memory.

Suffer, evolve, and fail.
Your fur, the extra teeth, the little tail

are almost gone. This is your curse:
that what is left also belongs to us.

THÉRÈSE: *DURCHBRUCH ZUM WEIB*

(Suicide, March 31, 1938, Vienna)

The room in the Kaufingerstrasse,
Sundays driving out of Munich
to the peaceful village of Dachau. . . .

Whose dreams followed more closely
the closed carriage, the walks in gardens:
his of women on their knees,

their faces hidden in their hands,
or mine of my own bad blood
flowing under the tight German words?

Even then our lives were in unseen hands,
each with a little puppet-face
nodding on a finger,

while the cities of Munich and Vienna
were being broken and reassembled
in the cracked mind of the painter.

What is the name for a woman
whose husband is "the Wolf-Man":
wolf-wife, woman, or wolf?

In your *Durchbruch zum Weib,*
what must the *woman* break through
while she waits to be found and taken?

Brought to Vienna to meet you
not for treatment but for approval,
I held your black eyes in my black eyes,

knowing their common origin
but never explaining it,
knowing I would have to explain it forever—

the mystery of ancestry
hidden in the lives of those who lie together
now, under a canopy of gas.

If I had been the patient
to whose dreams you fastened theories
like metal tags to pigeons,

news they cannot know,
would you have guessed the secret
poised outside my window?

So that space between us
keep unshattered and still,
what must we tie down?

You who rescue
dreamers from dreams
dream of me now

while I am fastening down the flag
which beats against the window
and waves at me to breathe and speak

and writing the note:
Do not light a match.
The air will explode.

FREUD IN LONDON   Summer, 1939

1

Behind me, my little statues of the gods
assume their placid, enigmatic look.
London might be Vienna in their eyes,
or Thebes—so anywhere is everywhere,
especially to a settled wandering Jew.
As in Berggasse, here the fixed arrangements
of meals and silent work among my totems
conceal a restless dreaming, as those trees
shelter this garden from the neighbors' houses.
What are those flowers? Names I cannot keep.
Their blues and purples burn through the afternoon. . . .
What will I dream of when I sleep at last,
or is there room for mine among the world's?
Isis, Osiris, Anubis, and Horus,
leave me alone, be with me. Are you dead?
Though we have grown around you and beyond,
you have set your judgments in our heads
like icy lights. Now, little gods, you stare
in one direction from the table, crowded
with books and objects, funerary stelae,
looking into the future from the past,
the look the dead have and the living learn
who know there is no present, only past
rolling itself uphill and down, a scarab
heavy with dung; the mind of Sisyphus.

2

A dog is barking somewhere in the garden
or somewhere in the house. My head is heavy,
I cannot tell where sounds are coming from.
My favorite chow, smelling the open wound,
no longer visits me. Life shrinks from life
if one no longer entertains the other.
This thought makes sense, and yet the mind confuses:
a child I know refused to start its labor
into the world, while I, at seventy-seven,
knew that I would never want to leave it,
island of pain in an indifferent ocean.
Kennst du das Land? On trips to Italy,
digging among its cropped and tumbled ruins,
I dreamed of Schliemann and his layered city—
did Troy know Troy as conscious knows subconscious?
Is each new love an old love with new language,
and at the heart of it, the heart deserted
and unbelieving still? What kind of hope
lies in the aging mind's forgetfulness?

3

Everything conscious wears away at last,
only what lies beneath remains unchanged.
I thought Vienna city of seductions,
city of wicked fathers, till I found
the daughters dreaming to become their mothers,
and sickened by their dreams. But when I worked
to bring them all to light, did I create
peaceable kingdoms in a wilderness
or anarchy in the world's eternal city?
This summer stretches toward the edge of nightmare;
it sees war coming, as a sickly animal
watches its foe approaching through the trees
and shuts its eyes. The sun is good. . . it sleeps.

Rome and Vienna are our prison cells
and yet we love the prison. Even here
where I was welcomed like an admiral
and where I came to die at last in freedom,
I miss the city that I said I hated,
thinking *at least they only burnt my books;*
such is the progress of our civilization.

4

Four legs, then two, then three: the riddle solved.
And if I choose to sit all day and stare
at flowers, have I any legs at all?
No voice, I cannot speak. A metal monster
to separate the nasal cavity
from mouth and teeth. Now cancer eats my gums.
People around me smile. Improve, improve.
I don't believe them, and I hate deception.
Soon I will say to Schur: the pain I held
at bay for sixteen years has overwhelmed me,
it makes no sense. Dear friend, give me the drug
and let me go. Today however—sunshine
reanimates the treasures on my table,
kindling my wishes, bringing me company.
The gentle poet HD, almost Grecian,
my visionary patient in Vienna
who saw victorious Nikes climb the walls,
and came to me for myths, not explanations—
she looked at all the objects in my room
before she looked at me. She sent me flowers,
or so I like to think. I see her now,
hiding her hands under the paisley rug
and glancing at her watch. The trouble was,
even so long ago, I was an old man,
she did not think it worth her while to love me.

5

Dali the Spaniard, candid and fanatical,
said that I had a cranium like a snail's.
It may be true. His eyes were like a snake's.
So animals, from their silence, reach and touch us
or look at us through windows in our heads
which open suddenly. Sergei the Wolf-Man,
when he had drawn a picture of the wolves,
exclaimed, "Herr Doktor, one of them is you."
And there I was, white-bearded, with black eyes
looking, and saying nothing. It took years
to show they meant no harm, and that their silence
was just the waiting for acknowledgement.
Is *homo homini lupus* in the end?
I said, "I have a grave philosophy—
you must have courage if you want to know it;
today we tunneled deep." And for that journey
it was enough that I was not alone
at every step; that when I looked around
a few were with me, watching and saying nothing,
making their thoughtful way across the snow.

THE SURGEON'S PHOTOGRAPH

1   April, 1934

Sun on the water. Six a.m. The loch,
rippling awake, shrugs off its raggy mist.
I point the lens where light, like lightning, strikes
bronze glitters from the forehead of a dark
primordial shape, who stirs and turns her head.
(My hand is steady: rewind, focus, click,
rewind and click and breathe in and breathe out,
check light, check water.) Graceful as a snake's
and forty times as large, the head inclines
toward Urquhart Castle, where a fisherman
calmly unloading tackle from a box
revolves his head toward mine and slowly nods,
finger to lips, as if he were a Merlin
and this were one of his shape-changing pupils.

Iguana eyes, the color of the water,
open and then stay open, looking through
and past me, saying simply, *I am here.*
For several minutes neither of us moves.
My neighbor looks at me as if I were
a new arrival from a moon of Saturn.
I focus, snap, and wind. My hands are steady
as if I held a knife above a vein,
ready to open passages beneath it
into the nervous world.
                          The sunlight makes
streaks like snakes across the water's surface.
I hold my breath. Sounding, the creature sinks
straight down, so quickly for that giant body
it seems her lungs must have collapsed at will,

propelling her to the bottom. As I watch,
my fingers moving with a separate mind,
I cannot tell precisely where I am.

I lost the beast. The camera caught the sun,
which rose and poised, as Venus rose and sank,
her bath completed or her view obtained
of little men who watched her from the bank,
one of them strange. I am not being witty:
she was as graceful and mysterious
as naiads bathing in a crystal bay
or forest, lit by ardent *chiaroscuro*:
watching her body reassume its darkness,
I felt my own withdraw into itself,
while the grey clouds, announcing heavy weather,
sealed the grey water in a tense reflection,
as if the landscape clenched against the sky,
and the dark gate which let me into mystery
had closed behind me, leaving me outside.

2   August, 1934

A clipping from *The London Daily Mail*:
"The lucky doctor, fishing in the morning
near Drumnadrochit, famous for its castle,
its salmon, and its single-malt Scotch whiskey,
captured the monster just as she was breaking
the surface of the loch two hundred yards
from where he stood. This is the only photo
the doctor would allow *The Mail* to publish."

True, there is something coy in secrecy:
who am I, after all? A London surgeon,
specialty: gynecology; age: thirty;
unmarried; six-foot-two, twelve stone or so;
a temper more inclined to melancholic
than saturnine; a desultory fisherman;
a sometime writer of descriptive prose;
nobody's husband, master-sergeant, valet,
lover, fiancé, confidant, or don,
just someone lucky with a camera—

Let me explain the reason for the secret.
That morning I had photographed four views
all from the same spot, finishing in an hour.
The fisherman I'd seen had disappeared.
Wrapping my mackintosh around the camera,
I packed it up and drove off carefully,
keeping the car at twenty. I kept looking
into the rearview mirror, as if she
(I call the creature *she* and never *monster*)
would rise up from the loch to claim her image
and repossess the magic in the box. . . .
Nothing went wrong. A reputable chemist,
G--- M--- of Inverness, agreed to print,
coaxing my negatives into the light.
We watched the photos swimming in their chemicals,
first streaks of grey appearing on the thick
white wetness like a sky through broken cloud,
and then—on (1), a crook of broken tree,
absurdly monstrous, floating in the water;
on (2), the dour face of the fisherman,
but seen up close, so close that one could tell
he had no teeth and one eye was a socket,
a face of simple malice, and on (3),
on (3), the figure of a naked woman,

the sun behind her brightening on her back. . . .
(G--- M---: "I don't git manny calls for this;
folks in these parts don't go for naikid ladies,
still, this is summat tastefuller than most.")
And what of (4)? On (4), a shadow wriggled,
shifted and chased its shadow in the brine,
and then assumed its form, as I had seen her.

A branch, a leering face, a naked woman:
how had these images usurped the pictures
I took of *her*? For it is clear I took them—
had I been dreaming, she would not appear
as here she does, in photograph and newsprint.
Thinking my actions backward like a film
rewound, unreeled, I take the first one. *Branch.*
A broken tree limb, looking like a monster
with the same arcing shadow for a neck—
well, it is possible my hand was shaking
(although I didn't notice) and I turned
the camera toward another floating shape.
(What if I did the same thing with a body,
delivering a woman of her bladder,
thrusting back the child into the cave?)
Go on. *The fisherman.* He had a calm,
serious visage, not this mask of cunning;
he looked at me with both eyes, undisfigured.
This face is like a devil's, only madder:
some local tramp who sleeps among the stones,
or mankie Celtic devil?
                         Now, *the woman*:
and here I feel the awful weight of telling
all that I know, for she is not a stranger,
and when I took the picture at the pool,
we were in Greece, and I was twenty-four,
and this, her body, with its longish curve

from waist to knee and heavy breasts suspended
by her two hands above the stirring water
and hair, wet, shining, flattened on her shoulders
in curling strips, has been now dead and buried
five years, although the five years seem like twenty.

3   July, 1978

Forty-four years of silence; forty-three
of this deliberate exile from the loch
declare, not war between me and my words,
but certainly a breach in testimony.
Do you imagine me an aging man,
his life curled up and dried around his vision?
It isn't so, and yet I find that facts
(a long, calm marriage, partially successful;
an easy doctor's life on Harley Street;
birth of a daughter, now a well-known scholar)—
that facts can lay a little line of stones
one beside one, across a breadth of water
and sooner or later, water rises up
to cover them again.
                                    A bright young man,
American, equipped with ideas and money,
wrote me the other day to ask advice
about the failure of his expedition
ever to get a single photograph
clear as the one I took so long ago
and quite by chance. (As quite by chance he'd found me
through old G--- M--- who thought me surely dead
by now and past the reach of local gossip.)
Pictures of oil slicks, upturned hulls of wrecks,
the back of a baby crocodile from Florida
put in the loch by someone as a joke,
a tantalizing and mysterious wash

from no apparent source, and once, a hump
traveling toward Foyers Bay at twenty knots,
and, inexplicably, some shots of beer cans
and *Playboy* centerfolds, and once, a beefsteak
two inches thick, char-broiled, with baked potato—
but never a shot to silence all the cynics
and quell the British Museum's staid *not proven.*

My daughter writes me that the Anglo-Saxons
believed the North Sea whale a sort of devil
who masked himself as land, to lure men's lines
and lash them to him as he dove *to halls
of death.* If something so disguised as land
can turn to a thing of water, cannot something
equally real turn into fantasy
without becoming any less the fact?
I'm thinking of that young man as I write:
his miles of sonar charts, and years of sightings
since Saint Columba, standing on the bank
mastered the beast with power of his voice. . . .
I am a doctor. I believe the legend.
And yet I see what happened long ago
to me was more an act of recognition
than one of faith, and that is how it must be:
not to believe in monsters but believe them.

You ask me of the woman in the picture:
she was my lover, and she died in childbirth
under my hands, which tried and failed to save her.
I know now how that picture came to light.
Although I don't expect you to believe me,
that young man might, whose work subsists on mystery—
There is a local saying that "the loch
never gives up its dead" and that is true,
but what then can it give up of its living?

A photograph, an image of the soul:
what could I give that image in exchange
but one of mine, a picture of a moment
I lived in first as fact and then as loss
and then as dream and now as memory
gone back to fact as to a ground of being?
As for the other pictures, of the branch
and of the hideous face across the bank,
I have no explanation but to guess
they are the creature's warnings of our fears,
of local superstitions and distortions,
but I don't know. I can't expect the loch
to yield all secrets now, and at this distance.

Summer again. Banked in the sweet sharp grass
above the northern shore, I train my Leica's
long lens and snap a calm, well-balanced picture
lit by the blue-grey light of summer evening.
Light on the water. Far away toward Foyers,
an expedition is loading up its vans
with cameras full of pictures of the loch:
Aldourie Castle, Dores, Bona Narrows,
and Borlum Bay where it is said two cops
spotted a baby monster in the shallows,
and Inverfarigaig, where "Water Kelpie"
rippled her back above the water's surface,
and Inchnachardoch where the creature stirred
waves of ten feet which flooded Cherry Island. . . .
And all that film, which *surely should have proved
something by now,* shows nothing, nothing, nothing.

THE STONE GODDESS

At Avebury in Wiltshire is a great henge which, together with the hills, barrows, rivers and springs in the countryside around it, makes a vast image of the neolithic goddess of fertility and the seasons. The body of the goddess provided places where stone age men and women could re-enact the cycle of the year; the four quarter-days mark special celebrations of the goddess as bride, mother, harvest-queen, and winter hag.

HENGE-WEDDING   (May 1)

Under the foxtail grass,
        under the cocksfoot and the greater-birdsfoot,
I am sleeping,
        the hillspur of my shoulder still in darkness.
When the sun wakes me,
        gleaming into the sockets of these skulls,
I will rise up with my big smile
        lively in the faces of my daughters.
Today, dressed in new skin,
        I will be goddess of the ox,
the white serpent who rolls over the hills,
        the ripple braiding the springwater;
goddess of clever fingers
        tying a hundred loveknots in an afternoon.
Now in my half-sleep I can hear you,
        women carving pots with flowing chevrons,
women gathering puffballs for their children's cuts,
        women of the Boss Cow
and the mouse named Prickeares,
        talkers and listeners,
and you who bend your face to the water
        stirring wrinkles into my face
and you who eat wild fern seed
        to make yourself invisible.

Today is your day.
        The lionhead sun has ordained it
and the oystershell moon whose body is full of surprises.
        Rise up with me and rub your eyes
and see yourself in time:
        the woman in the barrow, her skull cleft open
in two perfect shells to catch the river
        when it goes underground in winter;
there I am as I am always,
        alive in everything you know.

Remember this when the blood comes down,
    the ox-eye rolls in silent pain,
when your children give up their bones for me
    and you sit, grey as a stone,
watching the sea for its toss of treasure.
    Remember, drinking the seeds of light,
as you listen to the breath of a stranger
    and take your first steps in the dance
that you must not look back:
    for today I am young and hungry
and men are like wheat in the sweep of my arm.

BIG SUNDAY   (August 1)

Hob Foxhead is a farmer of wind,
refusing the first fruits to his neighbors' children.
No one will give him axes for his sheep,
he will go fireless in the winter twilight.
Still, he is a fine chunk of a man
whose red beard should somewhat excuse his temper
since it shows he is a cousin of the sun.

Daylight has swept the smoke from the beehives,
the honey pots are full, and under the alders
ten will be set to ferment as the summer
shortens toward the time of wingless ants.
Now I can see the line of visitors
threading around the hill where Beacon Stone
summons them yearly from their northern circle.
Everyone comes to us. It is the custom,
for no one can boast a hill as high as ours
or magic streams, or bees that make such honey
one taste of it will set an old man dancing,
or crickets that let you hear where you can catch them
to roast them on the rocks with salt and butter.

Last night I split the sky with lightning-laughter.
The men were drunk after a day of trading
and some new weed the women put in the beer
to see what happened. Nine of the farmers danced
until old Trippet pointed at the moon,
saying they'd turn to stone if they danced on Sunday.
All wore their faces blue, as is the custom,
with a big eye in the center of the forehead,

69

and one had eaten antler-root in barley
to see if he could stay erect all night.
Today, three of the women can't stop smiling.

After the storm I settled down to dream
the future-dream granted me by the harvest.
Most often it is babies, sheep and cattle,
a lot of open mouths I have to feed
and sometimes when the sky is a frozen cave
that will not yield its darkness, it is skulls
and little leg-bones bent in the shapes of sickles
and infants curled back underground like snails.
But this dream that I had was like no other.
A man in black was digging at the stones
who shouted at him, though he could not hear,
and others wearing tall funnels on their heads
were marching in a line into the hill.
I could not find my daughters anywhere
and all the dead were laid away in boxes
as if they'd done some crime against the earth
who would not let them lie down naked with her.

How cool these August shadows have become.
The reddening sun buzzes in the haystacks
like a sleepy fly; soon the old earth will take me,
its darkness sliding up to seal my mouth.
My dream, you swim under me like a shadow
watching the swimmer beat against the light
until its flakes dissolve around her limbs
and sleep is a mirror, lit with strange wet eyes.
If I could pray to time I would pray for sleep
blank as the sky in snow. . . but time is in me
like the memory of sunlight in the stones
and every dream that twists among the hills
I shall take in, as I lay down my head.

HAG-RIDDLES   (November 1)

I am beautiful, but only in my bones.
When they are visible, men hide in me.

I have three voices: the voice of thirst
like birds flapping in a cage of sticks,

the voice of storms, like fire roaring in a rock
or the moon calling for its lost light,

and the voice of silence, where whispers wander
looking for the names of the winds.

I live in a house
with no outside

on the edge of everything
though people always speak of me.

I teach them to curse
with the right side of their brains

and with the left
to learn how to sleep in ice.

I wear an invisible coat
with many soft pockets

each with a stone
which turns into a snake if you speak to it.

When I find that you have forgotten me
I rejoice

though I never forget myself
or the million names of my children.

If you want to see what I look like
draw a circle on a clean white rock

and stand there at noon on the shortest day.
Look at the rock until you see your shadow.

Your head will be bigger than the sun.
The shadow will never leave you.

BRIDE'S DAY   (February 1)

(Bride: pre-Christian goddess of the seasons)

Last night my stones ran down to the water
to drink. Their footsteps woke me
and when they came back and saw me with my open eye
they said, mamma, there is water in the spring,
you can see the wild grass moving.
I would have known it anyway. I always know.

It was a good winter. My storms did not fail me,
not Pecker, Whistle, Sweeper, or Complaint.
The birds raked the air with noises
like the sounds of chains in the leaves.
And the sun shrank as I told it to do,
sitting on the world's edge like a little gold monkey.

And the gifts were good: the braids of wheat,
the dark dresses for my disguises,
the ear-bones of the dead children
to help me listen for the first water.
It was a fine winter. I was uglier than ever,
they said they had never seen such a hag.

Now my thirst is going away, like a smoothed wrinkle.
Years and bad dreams are dropping from my life,
and the sun is getting bigger—
how could he help it, the way I look at him?
Soon I will have animals to carry messages,
and the world will be a round barn,

with four doors for the peaceable cattle,
and measured by the people in a circle
taking the average of their linked arms.
Soon I will be younger than ever
but wise as the day I grew old
teaching the trick of sleeping to the snakes.

Then you will stay all night with me
and waken with new words under your pillows.
What shall I make of you? Don't ask.
Touch me. Put all your arms around me
and when you sing in your sleep
I will turn the dew to pearls in your mouths.

ACP 0133

PS
3569
N5
F76
1981